I0481291

INBOUND
MARKETING
The Revolution Simplified

Patrick Bugeja
Founder of Intraforce Marketing

ISBN – ISBN-13: 978-1983738784
ISBN-10: 1983738786

Intraforce Marketing
http://www.facebook.com/groups/IntraforceMastermindGroup
http://www.intraforcemarketing.com.au/

"If you have more money than brains, you should focus on outbound marketing.

If you have more brains than money, you should focus on inbound marketing."

-Guy Kawasaki

Dedication

*I would like to dedicate this book, to my
beautiful partner and best friend, Carmela.
Her faith in God, patience, and believing in me
has given me the strength to carry on
regardless of the hard times.
She makes the path clear on those cloudy days.*

Introduction

If you own a business, any business, then you are a marketer. It doesn't matter if you provide a product or a service, your job is finding customers to purchase what you offer. Marketing can appear to be a complicated and devious process of convincing people that they need or want what you have, and you have what they want or need. The truth is that marketing plays a key role in economic and innovative progress. It is the fuel that drives invention, innovation, and research. Marketing is the way most people discover what is available to improve or enhance their life in some way. It is a reflection of how our culture and society evolves.

Despite the significant role that marketing plays in informing and introducing people to their multitude of options, it remains a point of resistance. Consumers, feeling bombarded by the onslaught of marketing and advertising to interrupt their day, have employed mental, physical, and digital shields to block marketing messages. This makes the job of a marketer, even more challenging.

That's why it is essential for all marketers to understand and embrace Inbound Marketing. Inbound Marketing is a game changer for any business enterprise. It is the most appropriate way to attract and engage with potential customers while providing helpful and valuable information to educate your prospects. Successful marketers know that an informed and aware prospect is more ready and available to learn about how your product or service can be the answer to what they are wishing or hoping for. And even more importantly, Inbound Marketing levels the playing field for businesses of all sizes. By using a high quality inbound marketing strategy, a small one-person internet business can compete head-on with multi-national corporations. The shift occurs when we align our marketing efforts on what matters to our prospects or target markets instead of focusing on what we have to offer.

Inbound Marketing is most effective when the goal is to serve and delight our customers. If we take the time to learn about what matters to them, to help them learn more about ways that our products or services can address their interests and needs, and we do what is necessary to nurture our precious client relationships, the results can be phenomenal.

No matter what you sell, Inbound Marketing can help your business to connect with more qualified prospects that are more likely to convert to customers. So, if you are ready to learn more about launching an effective inbound strategy, this book will show you how.

Table of Contents

"Our job is to connect with people, to interact with them in a way that leaves them better than we found them, more able to get where they'd like to go."
– Seth Godin

Chapter 1
The Evolution of Marketing

The practice of marketing is not a new concept. In fact, marketing (the process of promoting and selling products and services), can be traced back to the time of antiquity. There is even evidence of branding and packaging, dating back to the time of Pompeii. Yet, despite its undisputed existence for centuries, it wasn't until the modern era, that the true power of marketing emerged as a driver of consumer activity.

Ancient Egyptian Trading Expedition

Early marketing activities were carried out by commodity traders, who simply traded what they had for what they needed on a one-on-one basis. Over time, these early marketing activities transitioned through stages shaped by technological advancement and production capability. The industrial revolution and the ability to mass produce items, ushered in a marketing arena in which production capability determined sales. There was a pre-existing demand for most items produced. Having a sales strategy was not a necessity.

Companies just had to bring their wares to market and yield sales based on their production. Competition and alternative options were not an issue.

Ads all over the walls of a train station. Circa 1870s

Eventually, market saturation in the pre-war early part of the 1900s, created a new challenge for marketers – competition. As consumers were presented with more options, alternatives, and choices, marketers had to work harder to get a customer's attention and sale. This, transformation of the marketing operation, helped companies to realize that all of their engagements with potential customers, such as press releases, public relations, advertising, sales efforts, etc. were all components of their marketing and should be evaluated and managed as a unit. Slowly, marketers began to think about the needs of the consumers they were marketing to.

These marketing efforts changed dramatically after the end of World War II, when many soldiers returned home from war and were ready to settle down and start a family. This significant generational transition launched an unprecedented baby boom from 1946 to 1964. This population boom and the accompanying boost in consumer spending, launched the Marketing Concept Era.

During this time period, in modern day marketing, companies developed an understanding that their sales success was connected to the needs of their potential customers. Their profit was dependent upon determining what products and services consumers needed and wanted. Customer satisfaction also played an important role in motivating consumer activity.

This era also featured some significant demographic shifts that shaped the marketing evolution. Families were at the heart of the transition. Market strategy focused on serving the needs of the family consumer. Many products were created that appealed to mothers, children, and families in general.

Consumer purchasing power was also amplified during this period with the growth of credit-financed purchasing. More luxury items were accessible, and televisions became a family staple. Marketers also realized that having the right **product** at the right **price** and offering it in the right **place** with the right **promotion**, also known as the 4 Ps, meant success.

Interruption & Outbound Marketing

This new consumer era was fueled by the use of interruption marketing. Interruption marketing is also defined as traditional outbound marketing. Promotional messages are determined and dispensed when the marketer decides, whether or not the consumer is interested or willing to receive them. Outbound marketers essentially interrupt a consumer and demand their attention. Consumers are forced to respond in some way to the interruption even if it is to delete it, hang up, turn the page, or turn the channel.

At the time, interruptive marketing methods worked. Consumers learned about new products and services by being bombarded with magazine and newspaper advertisements, radio and television commercials, billboard ads, direct mail, and telemarketing calls. And when internet technology evolved so did the methods of interrupting. Unsolicited email spam was added to the outbound marketer's arsenal.

Television advertising was particularly alluring. By the early 1960s, about 90% of households had a television. By the late 1960s and early 1970s, color television was a common staple. This exciting new technology was a magnet for consumers who devoured this cutting-edge entertainment device. Both programming and advertisements enjoyed dedicated and attentive viewers.

By design and nature, interruption marketing lacks efficiency and economy. Often ads are distributed without optimal demographic targeting. Outbound efforts are often costly with low rates of conversion. However, despite the cost and inefficiency, outbound marketing worked then and still works today, albeit with less than optimal results or conversion rates. Some companies still use only interruption marketing to connect with potential customers. And many still use outbound interruptions as at least one part of their overall marketing strategy.

However, the biggest challenge to outbound marketing campaigns is nullification. Over time consumers have evolved in how they receive and react to interruption efforts. A significant amount of interruptive advertising is disregarded and ignored. Consumers are repeatedly bombarded by thousands of outbound efforts and have learned  to tune out massive amounts of low-value marketing message noise.

Even in the age of technological advances in outbound messaging delivery (such as pop-up ads on websites) there are equally tech savvy counter efforts (such as ad blockers) to help consumers shield themselves from unwanted and unsolicited marketing messages. Consumers have shown an expanding resistance to unwanted outbound marketing communication. This growing trend in consumer empowerment is what propelled the evolution of permission-based marketing.

Permission-Based Connections

In 1999, marketing strategy genius, Seth Godin, released the book *Permission Marketing: Turning Strangers into Friends and Friends into Customers*. This simple yet disruptive insight, launched a new era for the marketing industry. In order to achieve optimal effectiveness, marketers needed to realize that going forward, their efforts should be consumer driven. Getting permission from the customer to engage in conversation and to eventually present them with marketing messages, became an essential factor in an optimal marketing strategy. A new age of marketing was born.

Marketers who have adopted permission-based marketing, have yielded measurable results and optimized returns on their promotional investment budgets. Their advertising efforts are more cost efficient, by focusing on those who actually want to receive their messages. Marketing efforts are more targeted and appropriate for the recipients.

Permission-based marketing in many ways has been fueled by the Internet Age. Consumers can subscribe to, and thereby choose to receive, a company newsletter and sales notices via opt-in email. They can sign up on a website to access specific content that they want to receive.

However, the most profound augmentation of permission-based marketing is due to the parallel emergence of social marketing. Consumers can follow their friends and favorite companies on social media platforms such as Facebook, LinkedIn, Instagram, Twitter, YouTube, etc. to receive exclusive shared content and news. In an instant, anyone can share their opinion and experience (positive or negative) with everyone that they are connected to on any social media platform.

The Internet-Age in many ways has empowered consumers to instantly impact the success or failure of a company's marketing efforts. Consumers determine what companies they want to communicate with and have a relationship with. And it is this emergence of an empowered consumer and client-driven relationships that sets the foundation for Inbound Marketing.

Chapter 2
Client-Driven Relationships

"Consumers want products that tell stories, have magic, and inspire."
-Yves Behar

A newly empowered consumer, capable of blocking unwanted promotional messages and the ability to selectively determine what companies can send marketing communication, is at the heart of client-driven relationships. This new environment and marketing mindset is built upon a marketer's ability to attract potential clients and get permission to build a relationship with them, to communicate with them, and to introduce their products or services as potential solutions to a consumer's needs or wishes.

Marketers quickly discovered that it is no longer about what they want to sell, but about what the consumer wants and needs to buy even if they don't know that  yet. Instead of low-value advertising, internet savvy consumers now want ideas, suggestions, and solutions. They want information, so they can make the best decisions and the best consumer choices. They want to learn about solutions to challenges that they may not have realized until learning about something that applies to them.

Marketers also face the precarious paradox of trying (to gently and respectfully interrupt), to get a consumer's initial attention so that they can then get the consumer's permission to send future communications. This might also involve the gathering of additional personal information, so that future content can be customized.

"Make your marketing so useful people would pay for it."
– Jay Baer

The Rise of Relevance and Inbound Marketing
So, how do you get potential consumers to find you, so they can give you permission to communicate with them, without interrupting them in a less-appealing outbound marketing way? Simple, you use relevant inbound marketing.

Today, inbound marketing is the gold standard for successful marketing strategy. It is all about attracting the customers that are interested in your products or services. It is helping customers to find you, like you, and trust you in a natural and organic way. It is, as Seth Godin described, all about turning "strangers into friends and then friends into customers."

That takes us back to the paradox of how to attract (INBOUND) your ideal target market without using unsolicited and interruptive (OUTBOUND) methods. The answer lies in the art of relevance.

The easiest way to build a client-driven relationship is to be relevant. You need to be the answers to your prospect's questions. You need to talk about the issues and topics that matter to them. You need to educate your prospect about what could and should affect their decision and what they need to know and understand for optimal results. You need to purposely share your knowledge and expertise so that prospects know you may have the solution they are looking for. In short, you need to be relevant to their concerns, interests, issues, and challenges.

As a potential Inbound Marketer, you must be prepared to invest the time in a courtship. Your prospect needs to have an opportunity to trust you and a willingness to connect with you and learn from you. This isn't about making fast sales pitches. This is about educating your prospects about the topics and ideas that matter to them. And it is this "connection" that opens the door so that a stranger, becomes a friend, and then possibly a customer. The most effective way to initiate and build this ideal and progressive customer relationship experience is by creating compelling content. In other words, you need to create content that matters to your target market and compels them to indulge in what you have prepared for them.

The Crave for Compelling Content

Let's remember that consumers are still exposed to thousands of daily marketing messages that they are working diligently to block out. This doesn't mean they don't want to know about your product or service. It just means that they want, or more so crave, compelling content that educates them about the industry and products or services that could bring them solutions to their problems. They don't want the sale pitch, they want the education to make a good decision. They want to "learn" about new experiences, new choices, and new solutions. And you need to serve their need for information while delivering it in a creatively compelling way.

"Content is anything that adds value to the reader's life."
- Avinash Kaushik

Creating compelling content is easier today than ever before. By using a variety of internet tools and resources you can create interesting, appealing, attractive, and useful content that helps to empower prospects to know more about your product or service and how it may impact their lives. It may also serve to prove that you and your company are the experts that have the answers that your potential customers are looking for.

As you'll learn more about in Chapter 3, your ideal target client has a persona or set of circumstances that make them a perfect candidate for what you are offering. In essence, you have the answer or solution for whatever pain point your perfect client is burdened with. If you have taken the time to thoroughly research what matters to your target market, then you'll know what their biggest challenges are. What do they stress over? What keeps them up at night? What do they worry about? The more you know about what matters to your client, the more you'll understand their pain points.

Once you understand their biggest concerns, creating compelling content is as simple as helping them understand and address those pain points. There is a conversation going on in your prospect's head right now. You need to connect with them by being part of THAT conversation. That gets their interest and compels them to be receptive to your content and conversation. This also makes it easier for prospects to find you and connect with you through inbound activity.

Even more exciting for marketers that embrace inbound marketing, is the return on investment of money and time. Some of the most effective inbound content tools are completely free to use. And the expanded tools are cost effective in targeting specific niches of customers that want to know the expertise and information that you have to share.

Among the tools used to create and distribute compelling content and to generate inbound customer relationship opportunities are:

- Blogs and articles
- Social media posts
- Infographics
- Ebooks
- White papers
- Websites
- Podcasts
- Webcasts/webinars
- Forums

These content formats, become even more compelling when they appropriately include the keywords and phrases that matter to your prospects. When you focus on your customer and what matters to them and then apply creativity in how you provide answers to their specific problems, you have the formula for inbound marketing success.

These various types of content, if serving the needs of your ideal target market, will drive interested traffic to your website, opt-in email list, landing pages, and other lead capture resources. They are then ready to be nurtured and directed to your sales team for follow up or directly to your offer or buy links.

It is important to understand that this content process is not a "one and done" marketing solution. In order to truly and authentically serve the needs of your potential customers, you must have a persistent and committed presence, so that WHEN your prospect is ready to confidently take the next step in their customer journey, they will easily be able to find you. And they can only do that if you are providing a consistent and compelling supply of relevant content.

Chapter 3
Inbound Marketing
Strategy

The first step in building a successful inbound marketing strategy, is to get very clear on who your ideal or perfect customer is and why they should need or want your product or service. It all starts with the customer. Before you can create relevant, creative, and purposeful content to attract your ideal prospects, you need to know as much about your ideal client as possible.

 This process is expedited with the use of buyer personas. This is where you either think of your best client or a fictional ideal version of what your best customer would look and be like. You then seek to determine as much about their habits, challenges, career, home environment, education, goals, desires, preferences, hang-outs, hobbies, etc. as you can.

You need to then be very clear and honest about why they would want or need what you have to offer. What motivates them to want what you offer? What do they need to know, to determine that you have the solution they seek? What makes your offer different and better than your competitors? Is this a reason that matters to your ideal client?

Once you are very clear on who it is that you serve and why they would choose you, you need to then understand their buyer's journey. How will the ideal client go from stranger to friend to customer? This all begins with knowing where the buyer is on the buyer's journey. Are they not yet aware that they have a problem that you have the solution to? Are they aware and currently considering the options available to them? Or are they at the decision stage? By knowing where your prospect is along the buyer's journey, you can create the content that is most relevant to the questions they are tackling. This will also define what you need to educate them about.

Understanding the Inbound Distinction
Once you know who you are talking to and what the conversation is that is already going on in their head (where they are in the buyer's journey) then you'll know what type of content will drive your inbound sales funnel. Rather than placing ads that you hope your prospect will see,  you will create content that they are searching for and want to read and view before making a decision.

The differences between these 2 marketing methods is very important. For example: let's assume your business sells equipment to help new parents to safety proof their home. Outbound marketers might buy a list of new parents from a list broker, then pay a printer to create an informational sales flyer, then pay staff to stuff the flyer in envelopes, and then pay to have each letter mailed.

This direct mail outbound approach requires an investment in information, services, and labor to execute. Yet the average direct mail response rate is around 2%.

Now the same company, could instead use an inbound approach by creating a series of safety articles, that educate parents on risk exposures in their home, followed by solutions to reduce the risks identified. 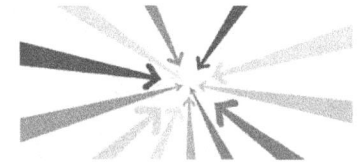 They can also then introduce their company's products that could help the reader to act on the safety education shared in the articles. This method, assumes that if relevant, useful, and educational information is shared it can drive consumer activity. This also, creates significant opportunities for companies with limited budgets, to level the playing field with a deep-pocket outbound marketer. On a very small creative and online budget, a small company can serve a large audience in a truly impactful and effective way.

Understanding Your Target Market

The most important factor in creating truly relevant content is to fully understand your target market. If you don't know what matters to your prospects, how will you create content that is relevant, compelling, and attractive enough so that your prospects find you before making a final decision?

One very useful tool to help inbound marketers to create truly relevant and impactful contact is to use buyer or customer personas. A buyer or customer persona is a fictional example of your ideal customer. By understanding who your ideal client is and what affects and motivates them, you can design and create content that is relevant to them. You can serve their needs and provide educational resources for them so that they are drawn to you.

In the 3 following examples of buyer/client personas, you can see how easy it is to imagine the perfect client or customer for YOUR business and develop a persona that reflects the circumstances that shape your perfect client's life. This helps you to "talk" to a real person with all of your marketing materials. Always "talk" to one perfect person. This doesn't mean that others who don't fit the exact client profile, won't do business with you. This exercise in planning helps to make sure your marketing activity is focused for effectiveness.

These personas can include different characteristics and data depending on what you should include in a profile of your perfect customer. When you create personas for your ideal clients, also document and consider how you can connect with them. How will they find you and connect with you? Are they on social media, the internet, etc.? This is important and will influence how you interact and engage with them.

Customer Persona #1
Best Customer - Sarah

DEMOGRAPHICS
A new 25-30 year old Mother of an infant or toddler. She is a stay at home mom. Her husband is the primary income producer. They have a household income of $65,000 to $95,000. They just bought a home in the suburbs of Boston with a big backyard for the 3 children they plan to have.

BACKGROUND/BIOGRAPHY
Before her baby was born, Sarah worked full-time as a customer service manager for a fashion store. She places high value on quality customer service and expects it from any companies she does business with. She also has a lovable German-Shepard mix rescue dog named Molly. She graduated with honors from Indiana University.

PSYCHOGRAPHICS, IDENTIFIERS,
GOALS, HOBBIES, INTERESTS, & ACTIVITIES
Even though Sarah plans to return to full-time employment, eventually, she right now is focused on building a family. She has also been considering the possibility of starting a small Shopify business from home so she has the flexibility to work and raise her children on a flexible schedule.Sarah is a vegetarian. She attends weekly Yoga classes. She plans to start a local chapter of Mommy & me classes for mothers of babies and toddlers in her community.

CHALLENGES, PAIN POINTS, & NEEDS
Sarah is worried about safety proofing her home for her young daughter and any "future" children she and her husband plan to have. She also thinks she's a horrible cook and worries that when her daughter is too old for baby food, she won't know what to feed her. She is skeptical of "quick fix" home safety services and worries that some prepackaged kid's food lacks the required nutrients.

COMMON OBJECTIONS, FEARS, &
REASONS THEY BECAME A CUSTOMER
She fears for her and neighbor children's safety. She looks for value when she shops. She is highly influenced by reviews and ratings. She does online research on most purchases, before she buys.

Customer Persona #2
Best Customer - Helen

DEMOGRAPHICS
Helen is a 58 year old grandmother and widow. She works as a registered nurse. She lives in Knightsbridge and works at a hospital in Chelsea, West London. She earns $75,000 pounds a year.

BACKGROUND/BIOGRAPHY
Helen is a breast cancer survivor. Her husband died 5 years ago of a heart attack. She has one son and 3 grandkids aged 5, 7, and 9. She has 3 cats. She has built a solid savings fund and is a few years away from retirement.

PSYCHOGRAPHICS, IDENTIFIERS, GOALS, HOBBIES, INTERESTS, & ACTIVITIES
Since her cancer experience and her husband's heart attack, Helen has made her health a priority. She exercises at a local community center 4 times a week. She also volunteers at a local clinic for low income women battling breast cancer. She loves to knit and attends weekly meetings of the knitters club. She enjoys traveling on cruise ships with her best friend. They take a trip each year.

CHALLENGES, PAIN POINTS, & NEEDS
Helen is worried about her health and independence. She is worried that as she ages, she might be safer in a senior living community. She needs products and services that will help her to maintain her health and keep her active as she approaches retirement. She is also worried that she doesn't have enough savings to support a comfortable retirement.

COMMON OBJECTIONS, FEARS, & REASONS THEY BECAME A CUSTOMER
She doesn't trust stockbrokers. She thinks that investing in the stock market is all a gamble. She will only invest in financial products that guarantee a return and the principal. She only buys products that have 5 star reviews or if they are recommended by a trusted friend or her son.

Customer Persona #3
Best Customer - Frank

DEMOGRAPHICS
A 40-45 year old single man. He was married and is now divorced. He has a 12 year old son from his first and only marriage. He is a sales consultant for a pharmaceutical firm in Sydney. He earns A$150,000 per year in salary plus commissions.

BACKGROUND/BIOGRAPHY
When Frank was in college he was a regional Golfing Champion and attended university on a sports scholarship. He has been dating a bunch of women since his divorce 5 years ago. But he would like to meet someone special and get married again.

PSYCHOGRAPHICS, IDENTIFIERS, GOALS, HOBBIES, INTERESTS, & ACTIVITIES
He loves to golf and on two weekends a month he spends the weekend golfing with his son. On other weekends he golfs with his mates. He also likes to travel to visit and golf on beautiful golf courses around the world.

CHALLENGES, PAIN POINTS, & NEEDS
Frank would like to find the perfect companion to travel and golf with. He is lonely right now. He also misses not being able to spend more time with his son. Frank is an adventure seeker and his biggest challenge is having the perfect companions to have adventures with. He also just learned that his employer might be merging with another firm that he has no interest in joining. So, he is worried about how a merger might affect his future. He is considering launching his own consulting firm.

COMMON OBJECTIONS, FEARS, & REASONS THEY BECAME A CUSTOMER
Frank is an easy going guy. He likes working with people and companies that think outside the box and embrace cutting-edge ideas. He expects honesty and clarity in any business dealings.

Now use the following Customer Persona Worksheet to start to describe your ideal target client.

Customer Persona Worksheet

DEMOGRAPHICS (age, marital status, occupation, gender, family details, geographic location, income, etc.)

BACKGROUND/BIOGRAPHY
(Education, life milestones, his/her story.)

PSYCHOGRAPHICS, IDENTIFIERS, GOALS, HOBBIES, INTERESTS, & ACTIVITIES

CHALLENGES, PAIN POINTS, & NEEDS

COMMON OBJECTIONS, FEARS, & REASONS THEY BECAME or MIGHT BECOME A CUSTOMER

As illustrated by these 3 sample client personas and your own sample client worksheet, once you know who you are talking to, who you are serving, what matters to them, and what they need to know, you can then create content that matters and is relevant to their needs. When you think of your potential clients as real people with real-life circumstances, you change the dynamic and potential of your message.

> *"Content is King but*
> *engagement is Queen,*
> *and the lady rules the house!"*
> - Mari Smith

It isn't uncommon for marketing staff to be tempted to take shortcuts in this step to prepare your inbound campaign. If you try to "talk" to too many people in your marketing messages (inbound or outbound) you risk essentially connecting with no one. Your marketing message effectiveness is strongly correlated to your ability to connect with a specific type of person with very specific pain points. You can't do that if your message is broad and casts a wide net. If your different products or services are perfect for distinctly different types of people, then create multiple types of content to connect to each group specifically.

This is key whether you are creating outbound or inbound marketing campaigns. You must know your client and the more you know about them, the more effective you'll be when you create your messages to connect with them. And when you get this part right, your prospects with be more likely to find you and more willing to learn more about what you offer to help them.

Chapter 4
Compelling and
Relevant Content

Have you ever been "slapped" by Google? That may seem like an unusual question, unless you have been involved in any online marketing, over the last decade. So, what is a "Google slap" and why should you care? And what does it have to do with creating relevant content?

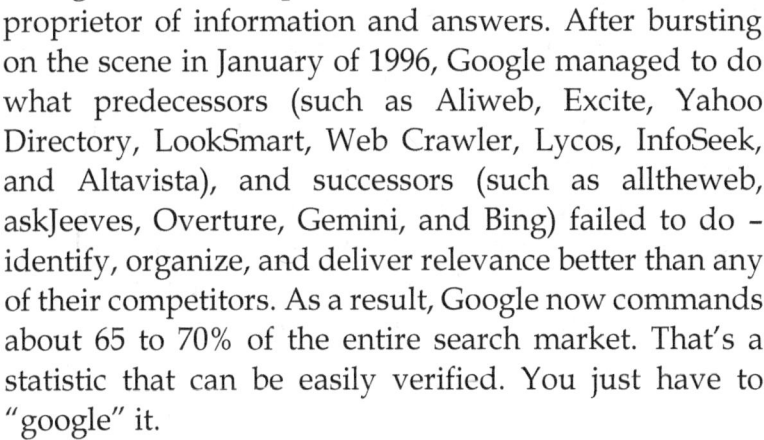

First, you need to understand how Google became so powerful in the search business. Over the last 10 to 15 years, Google has emerged as the quintessential proprietor of information and answers. After bursting on the scene in January of 1996, Google managed to do what predecessors (such as Aliweb, Excite, Yahoo Directory, LookSmart, Web Crawler, Lycos, InfoSeek, and Altavista), and successors (such as alltheweb, askJeeves, Overture, Gemini, and Bing) failed to do – identify, organize, and deliver relevance better than any of their competitors. As a result, Google now commands about 65 to 70% of the entire search market. That's a statistic that can be easily verified. You just have to "google" it.

Over the last two decades, we have had a front row seat, watching the evolution of indexing and accessing, massive amounts of information, on demand. Each of

Google's search company competitors experimented with various technological advancements in an attempt to identify an optimal strategy for organizing the unthinkable amount of information available (more on this in a bit) throughout the world. Just as challenging was the pursuit of a monetization strategy to support the maintenance of viable operations.

Despite some highly competitive strategies and innovations, by other search engines, Google emerged with a sequence of efforts that proved to be the "perfect" formula for organizing the world's information. They developed or improved upon algorithms, semantics, no-follow tags, filters, and pattern detection. And somewhere along the way "Google" became a verb. If there is something you need to know, all you have to do is "google" it!

Why Relevance Is Critical to Inbound Success

Any search result is only a good search result if it is truly relevant and represents the most appropriate and reliable sources on the topic searched. This includes both organic search results and top of page advertising results. In keeping with their corporate mission to: "organize the world's information and make it accessible and useful," Google's biggest challenge was relevance. This applied to advertising as well. So, Google's ongoing efforts have included several attempts to, "take out the trash" and keep search results on point and, of course, relevant.

Over the last decade, as advertisers and marketers have attempted "black hat" techniques to try to "trick" the

Google search engine to think their content is relevant, Google has countered with updates (namely Panda and Penguin), algorithms, filters, as well as trust and editorial value indicators, to nullify or block irrelevant results. This also, resulted in many tricky advertising and content violators, getting "Google slapped" and blocked from Google's prime advertising structures - Adsense, Adwords, and search results.

This empowered Google to literally block a business (that used "black hat" tactics to "game" the system) from access to their advertising network. This also included Google's ability to bury an irrelevant and low-value website content so deeply in the search results that no one would ever find it. And this is probably the best news that any legitimate and well-intentioned business could receive. What this essentially does is – level the playing field. Even a solopreneur on a very low budget, can create an amazing array of valuable and useful content that gets featured organically on the most coveted page one of Google search results for their keyword or topic.

As an inbound marketer, understanding how to appeal to Google search filters is paramount to your success, since about 70% of search traffic, comes from Google. And Google has made it abundantly clear that quality, clarity, value, and relevance matter.

You also need to realize that you are competing with an enormous and unthinkable amount of content. Looking at the most basic statistics, the amount of websites in existence, since the 1st one in 1991, has grown to over a billion. Those one billion plus websites amount to over 30 trillion web pages of content. And every minute of every day an unimaginable amount of additional content is created via posts (on Facebook, Twitter, Instagram, Tumblr, and Reddit, etc.), videos (on YouTube and Vimeo, etc.), reviews (on Google, Yelp, and Amazon, etc.), and pins on Pinterest – just to name a few. Google performs an estimated 100 billion+ searches every month.

So, how do you create compelling and relevant content that appeals to Google search? It all starts with your customer.

"Google only loves you when everyone else loves you first."
– Wendy Piersall

Creating and Repurposing Content that Matters

As we mapped out in the last section, it is imperative that you know and understand what matters to your ideal clients. Much of what is important to your ideal clients, is revealed as you create your client personas. What are they worried about? What do they care about? What are their wishes, hopes, and dreams? How do they like to learn new things? What matters to them? What are the answers to their questions? How can you help them on their customer journey to clarify their needs, know their options, and make educated decisions?

First and foremost, your content must be relevant to their concerns, interests, issues, and challenges. What piece of guidance, advice, or tools can you share digitally in exchange for the opportunity to build a relationship and connection with them? And how do you make your content compelling so that it is user friendly, easy to digest, interesting, useful, educational, noticeable, visually appealing, and has a purpose - to bring value to your target market?

Armed with your customer personas (see Chapter 3) and an understanding of their buyer's journey, first plan and determine what information would be appealing and helpful to your ideal customer. Then determine what types of content formats, would be most helpful to deliver that  information. In most cases, the same content can be re-purposed in many of these formats. Some possible content options include:

- Audio content
- Blog posts and articles
- Case studies
- Checklists
- ebooks
- Infographics & images
- Slide presentations
- Research reports
- Social media posts

- Teleseminars
- Templates
- Videos
- Webinars
- White papers
- Worksheets and lesson sheets

The most compelling and optimal choice of formats you make are dependent upon how your ideal customers choose to get their information.

For example: let's assume that your target client group, based on individual personas, spend a great deal of time watching educational YouTube videos. They are visual learners. You can create a quick instructional YouTube video, to teach your prospects about 1 small aspect of their primary concerns. In order to create this instructional video, you'll prepare a script to be used in the narration of the video.

You can then recycle/reuse (or repurpose) that video script as a PDF handout, for those who are verbal learners and like to read content. For your aural learners you can create an auditory file, (podcast or mp3). You can take it a few steps further by using your video script to create a PowerPoint presentation to submit to SlideShare or use the visuals to create Pinterest posts. There are many additional ways to expand your reach by reviewing the content list above. The key is to realize that if you have some interesting content, you can optimize the value of that information by using it to create multiple types of content.

The Words & Topics That Matter to Your Clients

Your content must also be "labeled" correctly with titles and headlines that include the words that tell your customers, "this is for YOU!" Part of understanding what matters to your target market is knowing the buzz words that are associated with their interests. The buzz words that might appeal to a new mom could be much different from the buzz words that will quickly get the attention of a teenager. Know your customer, know what topics and information matters to them, know what visual images get their attention, and know the words that they use and respond to. This knowledge will guide you and your team to create the content that your customers need and want. You will know where they look for such content and the formats that work best for them.

"Focus on the core problem your business solves and put out lots of content and enthusiasm and ideas about how to solve that problem."
-Laura Fitton

Let's take a look at the various types of content that can be created to serve a sample client.

MARKETER PROFILE: A Real Estate Agent

SAMPLE IDEAL CLIENT: Young couple with a new baby or toddlers, purchasing their first home.

SAMPLE CONTENT:

- Blog posts and articles – *5 Traps You Need to Know about Before You Apply for a Mortgage*

- Checklists – *10 Documents You Need to Have Ready and Up to Date Before You Apply for a Mortgage*

- Books/eBooks – *Buying Your First Home – The Step-by-Step Process*

- Infographics – (see image on next page) *Awesome Things You Can Do When You Buy a Home*

- Social media posts – Images and tips for new homebuyers with pictures of happy families in a beautiful home setting with plenty of room.

- Checklists – *7 Steps to Buying Your First Home*

- Videos – *How to Inspect a home for damage BEFORE you make an offer*

- Webinars – Teach a class online about how to apply for a home loan

- Worksheets and lesson sheets – *Filling out a loan*

application step-by-step

As you can see, there are many types of content that can help your potential customers. The key is to create the content and get it out there. This content can be posted on a company website as well as posted to a variety of online content sharing sites like YouTube and Pinterest and shared on social media.

"Make the prospect a more informed buyer with content."
- Robert Simon

Social Resonance, Significance, and Influence
Content that compels your target market, is about them and their needs and interests. It isn't about you and your products, but about the solutions and answers that your clients need. When your content compels your target market to take notice, you might also benefit from your target market's own social network. When you provide value to your target group, they will likely share the knowledge and insights with others that are in their circle of influence. So, relevant high-value content that serves your target market is also highly beneficial to your business, especially when your target market shares your content with their own social networks of influence.

In addition to the primary benefit of getting your prospect's attention and earning access to their network of influence - is the essential "stamp of approval" from social proof. As we discussed in Chapter 1, in an instant, anyone can share their opinion and experience (positive or negative) with everyone that they are connected to on any social media platform. This is the power of social influence and consumers by alerting their personal social networks, can make or break a brand by setting off a chain reaction of messaging like a flick of the first domino in a falling row of dominos.

Social influence is also empowered by reviews. Every day, individual consumers post reviews on Google, Yelp, YouTube, Amazon, and more. And these reviews can either make or break a product or company. This is further enhanced by the social media shares of the reviews and other review sharing opportunities.

The impact of this power to influence, validate, and promote, socially, is something that Google assigned great weight to. So, this too will boost your search engine value. And for all of these critical reasons, compelling content functions as the driving force behind an inbound campaign.

Chapter 5
Search Engine Optimization (SEO) and Social Proof

*"The best place to hide
a dead body is on
the second page of Google search."*
- Anonymous

At this point, many marketers wishing to transition or launch a business with inbound marketing might be overwhelmed by the challenge. With over a billion websites and over a trillion web pages, the looming question is – How will your customers find your business among TRILLIONS of options? In short, the answer is by **optimizing** your **relevant** content for search engines (i.e. **Google**) and by **social proof.**

How SEO Drives the Search Engine Process
First, let's talk a bit about what search engine optimization (SEO) is and then how it has evolved in importance and impact as search engines were developed and refined. In its most basic form, SEO is the process of optimizing a website or webpage so that is has an improved likelihood of being found and ranked well by search engines. SEO refers to the natural, organic, or unpaid search results that a search engine determines are the best matches for a specific search query. The

higher a site's appearance on a search engine results page (SERP) is directly correlated with the amount of traffic to the sites featured. So, SEO is the driving force behind a site's ability to be found among the trillions of pages on the web.

Ever since the first search engines were created in the early 1990s to document and index the growing volume of files and pages on the web, the challenge has been to deliver or return the most relevant results to any query. By the mid-1990s, marketers realized that information on websites could promote a business and drive sales. Some early SEO pioneers are credited with building connections and knowledge sharing among developers to tackle the ongoing challenge to improve search results. And as search engines continued to evolve in indexing and organizing volumes of content, information, and documents, developers worked to improve the relevancy of the results.

SEO was in some ways the result of pure economics. As the realization came to light that business could be generated on the internet and that more traffic meant more potential customers and more revenue, traffic become paramount. And traffic was a direct function of ranking in search engine results. So, the new challenge was how to optimize a webpage so that it was more easily found and identified as a top match for a search query.

Once marketers discovered this search engine rank to traffic to revenue link, things started to get ugly. Marketers attempted to do whatever seemed effective to "trick" search engines to think a specific site was an optimal resource to match a specific query. This led to the practice of Black Hat SEO, which basically described aggressive efforts to influence a site's ranking using deceptive or sneaky tactics that were not focused on the needs of the end-user (those looking for relevant information).

These marketers would create massive fabricated networks of links to make a site appear more important, popular, or influential than it was. They would fill (actually stuff) a page with irrelevant keywords to make their sites appear to be something that they were not. Imagine that you needed a haircut. So, you walk down the street and see a sign that says barber shop. You then go inside and discover that the sign was a lie. Inside was a tattoo parlor. And now instead of a haircut (that you really want) someone is trying to convince you to get a tattoo.

As you can imagine the chaotic state of search at the time, made it difficult to find relevant information. In fact, this search engine mess is what inspired 2 Stanford students (Sergey Brin and Lawrence Page) to create

Google. And Google changed everything. At first, the goal was to create guidelines for White Hat SEO. This meant actions and factors that the "good guys" would use that supported value, quality, and relevance for the end user. However, the lure of revenue from Black Hat tactics did little to inspire White Hat actions.

As a result, Google focused on enhancing their search engine algorithm to weed out and "punish or hide" irrelevant and deceptive sites and reward (show up in search results) sites that truly delivered results that were high quality and on point. As documented by MOZ (**https://moz.com/google-algorithm-change**) Google maintains an ongoing attempt to adjust their algorithm to maintain optimal search quality.

This, of course, begets the question, what is Google looking for, now? Despite the many algorithm changes and tracking by strategists, Google's exact algorithm indicators are unknown. It is believed that Google uses over 200 factors to determine relevancy and they are a closely guarded to protect against Black Hat efforts to game the system. However, many SEO strategists have determined some of the most likely quality indicators that are known to boost and influence SEO. One very creative summary of best practices was created by Search Engine Land as a periodic table of SEO success factors. See: (**https://searchengineland.com/seotable**).

There are several factors that we know drive search engine results and are best practices for achieving optimal placement in search engine results. And remember, this natural and organic discovery of relevant and high-quality information is what fuels an inbound marketing strategy. Search engine diligence is an inbound marketers best friend. It means that if you produce high quality content that truly serves your ideal customer, then the chances they will find your content when they are searching for it, are greatly improved – or optimized!

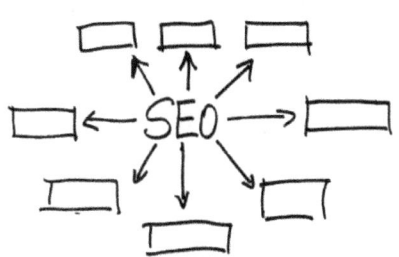

"Better content is outweighing more content."
– Rand Fishkin

Google, takes their commitment to delivering quality search results very seriously. They start by first trying to figure out exactly what you mean. The algorithm will correct your spelling, finish your search string, and give you potential options to finish your search description. They will even use synonyms to correct the word you likely meant to type. Then the algorithm goes to work to deliver the most relevant results to answer your query along with some appropriate ads that also match your query, because Google has to have a way to pay for their "little old free search machine."

Some known factors that boost Search Engine Optimization:

- Geolocation – So, if you search for barber shops you will see a list and some ads for barber shops near you.

- The quality of a website as determined by the overall quality and quantity of good content.

- The freshness of content and websites. Is it regularly updated with new information (for example the publishing of frequent quality blog posts)?

- Labeling – this means that the structure of the content is coded with accurate tags, labels, and descriptions to tell search engines what the webpage is about.

- The content organically and authentically utilizes the keywords that are appropriate for the content so that searchers can connect with that content by searching for the same key words.

- Social Proof (as described in Chapter 4)

How Social Proof Influences Search Results
Social proof refers to the role that content sharing plays is endorsing and scrutinizing content. The assumption is that humans have a natural tendency to share good,

interesting, and useful information. In the "old days" this would be as simple as telling your friends and family about a product or service that you tried and really liked (or disliked). It could be a recipe or a remedy for stain removal. Anything and everything is shared with others in some way.

"Content is fire,
social media is gasoline."
- Jay Baer

However, this simple concept of influencing your personal network took on an amazing new dimension with the onset of social media. In seconds we can now share with thousands of connections our pleasure and displeasure with just about anything. And within a few more seconds everyone in our network can then share that insight with everyone in their own social networks. Each and every consumer now holds the power to make or break a business or brand in seconds. Google's algorithm gives value to these individual content evaluations whenever online content is shared. The more a content item is shared, the more it is believed to be information that others may also find relevant.

"A brand is no longer what
we tell the consumer it is -- it is what
consumers tell each other it is."
– Scott Cook

Successful inbound marketers focus on the value of expediting and nurturing social sharing. The goal is to serve your target market authentically and earn access to the social network of influence that each individual customer controls. So, if we revisit the question, "how do you create compelling and relevant content that appeals to Google search?" It all starts with your customer and then it can extend to their entire social circle of influence.

Chapter 6
Inspiring Action with Quality Content

"Content builds relationships.
Relationships are built on trust.
Trust drives revenue."
- Andrew Davis

Once you have a clear understanding of what content would be most appealing and compelling to your target market, the ultimate goal is to inspire them to take action. The primary tool to inspire action, is the Call to Action.

The Importance of a Call-to-Action (CTA)
The primary purpose of content is to attract and serve your potential customers. The more your content meets their needs, the more likely they are to be interested and willing to engage with your content. The secondary purpose is to encourage them to take action to engage with your organization. You might want them to place an order, set up an appointment, call in to your company to talk to your sales team, opt-in to your newsletter, write an online review, recommend your product, etc. The most effective way to get them to do any of these things is to create a compelling and clear - call to action.

In many cases, the marketing objective is to compel the prospect to click a link in your content that takes them to a Landing Page where they will have the opportunity to view your call-to-action offer. This might be your newsletter opt-in page to capture the lead into your prospect database – or sales funnel. It might also be an outright click taking them to your order page.

So, your compelling and relevant content will drive traffic to your landing page where visitors will view your offer or opportunity and experience your call to action. After your client clicks on your content and website, they are then taken to a Thank You page or your upsell/down sell page.

Your Content > Landing/CTA Page > Thank You/Respond

A Call-to-Action Example - the Process
You run a resume design company. You know that people are more likely to design a new resume when they are looking for a new job. Your content (for example a blog post) talks about how to ace a job interview by knowing the most frequently asked interview questions. This content appeals to a target group of people who are looking for new jobs. This is important content for those who are seeking better employment opportunities and a successful hiring process.

At the end of the blog post, a Call-to-Action could be the opportunity to receive a "cheat sheet" of the best answers to the most common questions that interviewers ask during a job interview. This is something that is expanded content and would be highly beneficial to your blog readers. It is a motivator and drives traffic to your Landing Page with a Call-to-Action offer button. If the reader clicks the offer button to receive the "cheat sheet," they will be opted into your company newsletter. This action has now attracted the new subscriber into your sales funnel.

After the readers, click on the call to action, they are taken to a Thank You page and receive instructions on accessing the motivation item that triggered the action.

Some examples of Calls-to-Action include:
- Call Now
- Donate now
- Learn more
- Start now!
- Download the ebook
- Get the eCourse or Starting Lesson
- Get started
- Get Exclusive access
- Get Your FREE Trial Now
- Get Your Exclusive Savings Coupon
- Reserve Your Seat
- Schedule an Appointment
- Get it today!
- Subscribe
- Try it for FREE
- Talk with a live rep, right now

> *"All action results from thought,*
> *so, it is thoughts that matter."*
> -Sai Baba

Features that Facilitate Action

Some of the most effective calls-to-action include some of these features:

- The Keys to a Successful Call-to-Action sequence is that the underlying benefit or reward for taking action must have value for the visitor. If the "reward" is content, then it must be a resource that is compelling to the target audience.

- The CTA samples above are in Second person. Some suggest that using 1st. person yields better results. For example: Get My FREE sample, Start my free trial, etc. Test both and see how your prospects react.

- The best landing pages are ones that only provide one possible action to take. Too many choices often hinder any action.

- They are best when they are one-page websites with minimal distractions.

- The Landing page should have an interesting but uncluttered design to maintain reader focus on the CTA.

- The CTA button should be at the top of the fold, bright, and obvious. A clean, neat page without unnecessary clutter.

- What might create hesitation with your prospects? Address that on your landing page with testimonials, a list of benefits, or other proof-related support.

- Be sure to have your landing page optimized for the devices that your prospects might be using. Mobile optimization is often overlooked.

- The CTA button or on page image, should inspire feelings of emotion. Use words that spark emotional reactions with your target group.

- FOMO – Creating an element of FOMO (The Fear of missing out) is also a strong motivator.

- Colors and numbers play a role in boosting emotional reactions. For example, RED is often associated with clearance sales. It creates a sense of urgency and pressure. Orange (as evident by Amazon sites) is an optimal color for BUY buttons. It also works well for a SUBSCRIBE button. Likewise, numbers grab attention: Only $99, Top 7 Short-Cuts for Acing Your ACT Exam, etc.

Once you have determined the right content to drive interest, the right call-to-action, and the best way to structure your call-to-action landing page, what remains is an appropriate way to gather your action takers. Some actions will require automation to deliver the "reward" for taking action. Other actions, may require staff to receive inquiries. The key is to be ready and prepared to respond to the actions that your inbound marketing sequence put into motion.

> *"Obeying a prophetic call to action brings positive benefits."*
> – Sherry K. White

However, no matter how many leads you get from the action takers and responders to your calls-to-action, they are only of value to your business if you have established a plan to capture, harness, engage, convert, and delight these new relationships. You need to have a clear vision of what your ideal customer's journey looks like. You need to have structured client work flows. You need to have a plan to capture and harvest your leads. This will be covered in depth in Chapter 8. But first, let's discuss disruptive marketing.

Chapter 7
Disruptive Marketing

"Disruption is all about risk-taking, trusting your intuition, and rejecting the way things are supposed to be. Disruption goes way beyond advertising, it forces you to think about where you want your brand to go and how to get there."
– Richard Branson

Before we discuss capturing your leads and CRMs, it is important to shed some light on the concept of Disruptive Marketing and how it could rapidly propel a company's marketing efforts and revenue. Despite the ominous description, disruptive marketing is great for business. What this describes is action that "disrupts" the way an industry has been operating, to create a new way of doing things, or a new market altogether.

The marketing industry itself is adapting to disruptive changes in promotional methods and strategies. Ongoing digital innovations and the integration of artificial intelligence have transformed customer experience, engagement, and automation.

Disruptive Innovations
In some situations, Disruptive Marketing might simply replace old technology with new technology. This would include situations where a company improves a

product or service with enhancements that improve efficiency, or timing, or reduce costs. It might be represented by a company that does things differently, a new product that disrupts the market and takes the lead, or by collaborations that yield optimal outcomes. It could also be a change that creates a whole new market segment. It is market-leading innovation at its core.

Successful disruptive marketers are innovators that understand the needs and challenges for their customers and their industry. They break through the noise to grab their clients with a surprising, relevant, funny, and/or an edgy twist on the old way of doing things.

Some examples of disruptive companies, marketers, products, and technology, include:

- Virtual Reality VR Marketing – A Virtual immersion allowing the customer to sample experience a vacation, driving a sports car, or engaging in an adventure has and will continue to transform the sales experience.

- A company called Give Vision is disrupting the vision options for those with vision limitations. Using a device similar to VR goggles, the screen can provide enhanced vision capabilities for vision-impaired patients.

- Airwick created a "Scent Decorator" quiz so customers could match the right scent to create the desired mood in their home.

- A Portuguese company called Faarm is disrupting the way we document food sources and traceability. This is especially critical in situations where livestock is contaminated and affected livestock must be accurately identified and located.

- A college grad disrupted the underwear market with a company called MeUndies. The goal was to create the world's most comfortable and sustainable underwear while utilizing a responsible manufacturing source. Add in some social proof from some great celebrity endorsements and you have a market success case.

- A company called Bump Mark is disrupting the food storage/spoilage industry by developing bio-reactive packaging labels that show when food is actually no longer safe to eat. This reduces food waste and illness from consuming spoiled food.

- A company called Codec, is disrupting the content marketing industry by using Artificial Intelligence to determine what content your prospects actually want to see and what content will be relevant to them.

Disruptive marketing can also be used to effectively connect and inspire social change. The Anar Foundation created an impactful outreach campaign to help abused children. Using height based lenticular technology, a message board presented one message and image to adults, ("*Sometimes, child abuse is only visible to the child suffering it*") and revealed a different one to children, ("*If somebody hurts you, phone us and we'll help you*"). The image in the child's view range was of a child with cuts and bruises. (https://youtu.be/6zoCDyQSH0o) The disruptive goal was to offer help to children who might be accompanied by their abuser. That is a innovative and impactful way to connect with guarded and vulnerable populations.

These are just a few examples of how companies are taking the lead in their industry by finding new ways to achieve new and better results. In many cases, these companies have themselves, relied very heavily on optimizing their inbound strategies to assure that they not only connect with potential clients but with potential investors as well.

Any company that has the insight and is fortunate enough to identify some way to disrupt the status quo in their industry or innovative enough to find a new market with a new in-demand product, will have an abundance of opportunities to create compelling and educational content to fuel their inbound marketing strategy.

The Value of Disruption
Disruptive developments aren't just important to your

company, they play a critical role in progress and innovation in virtually every industry and market sector. What would the world be like if someone didn't push for motorized vehicles vs. horse drawn buggies, or electric light vs. candle light? Whenever there is thought "outside the box" amazing things are developed that make life "inside the box" more interesting and enhanced. Some companies that were built on foundations designed to disrupt their industry include Apple, Amazon, Uber, and Netflix.

> **"If you double the number of experiments you do per year, you're going to double your inventiveness."**
> -Jeff Bezos

So, is there a new perspective possible in your line of business? The more you understand your industry and your customers, the better chance you'll have to identify how to turn the industry upside down with a new product or service, or a new way of doing things.

Chapter 8
Capturing & Nurturing Inbound Leads

"What you plant now,
you will harvest later."
-Og Mandino

So far, I have outlined the power of building an inbound marketing foundation for your sales and promotion endeavors. I have also shared some essential insights about the importance of creating compelling client-centered content to fuel your inbound strategy. And I have explained the factors that determine the relevance of your content and why that matters.

However, all of this knowledge and understanding is worthless if you haven't mapped out your client's journey and your client workflow from prospect to client. You also need to clearly define the stages and sections of your sales funnel.

Building Your Inbound Sales Funnel

A sales funnel is the hypothetical path that your prospects journey through on the road to becoming a customer. Sales folks like to describe a device shaped like a funnel where the mouth of the funnel is the largest part of the opening, ready and available to allow an adequate amount of leads to enter the process.

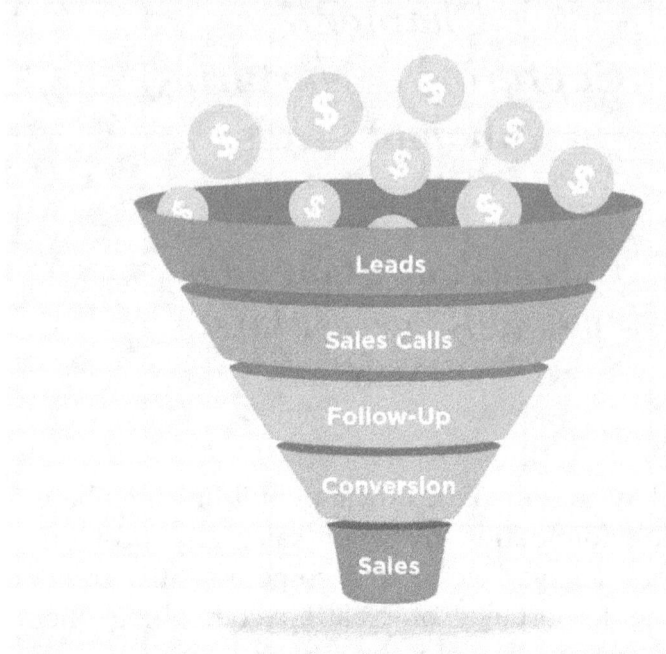

Initially these leads or prospective clients enter your sales funnel after encountering some content with a call-to-action of some sort. They might be responding by signing up for your email list in exchange for receiving some informational product that you used as a lead magnet. Your lead magnet is most effective if it clearly attracts and appeals to your target client group.

As there are opportunities to engage these prospects, some are sufficiently nurtured to progress through the funnel to be more likely to convert into "hot" leads. And then from that group, a smaller segment travel to the base of the funnel and become customers.

In reality, your sales funnel might be vertical, linear, or another type of path. That's not important. What matters is that you are very clear on **your** customer's buying journey. You need to have a very clear understanding of how they should transition (knowing all of the steps and qualifiers) from lead to customer. And you need to have a system in place to both capture and nurture your leads.

Email Lists, CRMs, and Autoresponders

Once you have created some compelling content to drive your INBOUND marketing campaign, you will likely attract organic traffic to your content. If structured correctly, your content will include some type of call-to-action. This might include actions such as:

- Contact us
- Call us
- Request Information
- Subscribe, Opt-in to an email list
- Download a report, eBook, white paper, etc.
- Take a survey
- Sign up for a trial

When your prospect takes the requested action, you need to capture that lead. One of the easiest and low-cost ways of capturing a lead is with an email list. A simple opt-in CTA will add a prospect to your permission-based email list. Once they are in your sales funnel, you can continue to email them updates and deliver engaging content to nurture your leads to eventually take a larger CTA to buy or become a customer.

The process of nurturing leads on auto-pilot is easily expedited with an email list autoresponder. This assumes that the obvious client progression is similar for most of your prospects. This means that all of your leads can receive the same series of follow-up messages after they begin their journey and are added to your sales funnel. An autoresponder will know that any new additions should receive the same series of follow-up messages that you map out when you set up your sales funnel.

Some larger organizations, that have a sales team to "work" the leads to facilitate customer conversion, might also use a Customer Relationship Management (CRM) software program. A CRM is a more robust prospect and client management tool that allows for the integration with the sales team to create a systematic process for engaging and converting leads to clients. We'll discuss this more in Chapter 9 on Smarketing.

The Value of Client Workflows

By automating as much of the client development process as possible, a company can reserve precious sales team time for the final stages of the client conversion experience. A CRM can track follow-up efforts and provide a  methodical approach to managing the traffic in your sales funnel. This assures that even when your organic traffic efforts are delivering an abundance of prospects, your CRM will be able to prioritize, while maintaining order and structure in your marketing systems.

Points, Scoring, and Sales Integration

One of the biggest challenges to companies that generate an overwhelming number of leads is to determine what leads, have merit and are the right inquiries to pass on to the sales team. In other words, how do they know which leads the sales team should focus their limited time and efforts on? The answer to this challenge is the use of points or some other scoring or categorization system.

The key to creating a successful lead scoring/points system is to integrate with the sales team at the early stages of the project. The sales team is in the best position to reveal what demographics, features, experiences, or actions, result in the best sales leads with highest conversions. When the marketing strategy team, works with the sales team, the chances of operating an efficient sales system, improve substantially.

For example:

You can have leads go through a funnel with a point system. Once they reach 100 points, only then they are qualified to send to the sales team. A possible point breakdown could be - opening the third email would earn them 50 points, responding is a further 50 points = 100 points. The goal is to incorporate actions that are more likely associated with sales quality leads.

What the sales team will be able to contribute is a profile of an ideal customer. This may include both explicit and behavioral attributes. Explicit attributes are demographics like job, career, age, gender etc. Behavior attributes are linked to the actions taken by the prospect. The marketing and sales team can then outline an arbitrary point system to nurture leads from TOFU (the Top of the Sales Funnel), to MOFU (Marketing Qualified lead, and then BOFU (bottom of the sales funnel – where the prospect becomes a customer). This is all necessary to nurture each valuable lead so that the ones that are convertible into becoming clients – do.

Chapter 9
Optimizing Results
with Smarketing

"Things get done only if the data
we gather can inform and inspire
those in a position
to make a difference."
– Mike Schmoker

Your company can create amazing content to fuel a super successful inbound campaign to gather an abundance of leads into your sales funnel. But, all of that effort is wasted if your marketing team is not integrated with your sales team to maximize the outcome with those leads. Engagement is useless if it doesn't provide your sales team with qualified leads when your prospects are ready to take action.

So how do you make sure that your best leads are at the top of the pile so your sales team spend their efforts on the prospects that are most-ready to take action? The short answer is...you use smarketing to assure that your marketing and sales teams are integrated for optimal outcomes.

Integrating Your Sales and Marketing Teams
Smarketing is a marketing term used to describe the integration of an organization's sales resources with its

marketing strategy, advertising, and other promotional efforts. When the sales team and marketing team, two significant drivers of business development are integrated and synergized, the result is an enhanced marketing operation with the potential to produce optimal results.

Neither segment can achieve its true potential impact on a business without the efforts and coordination with the other. If marketing is wildly successful in generating leads and identifying qualified prospects but the sales team poorly follows up with those leads, or worse, never contacts them – then significant resources are wasted, and revenue is lost.

Likewise, if the sales team is trained and ready to connect with qualified leads but there are not enough leads to keep them busy, then again – resources are wasted, and revenue is lost. Keeping these two key drivers of revenue in optimal balance helps to create optimal yields in revenue.

The deliberate effort to achieve synergy and integration of these two critical contributors to business growth is regarded by many marketing strategy experts as an essential component to a successful marketing action plan. Often this merging, of sales force resources and marketing insights, is regarded as not only strategically advantageous but also essential to an organization's success. Organizations that are committed to optimizing their resources, efforts, and outcomes must embrace "Smart Marketing" tactics which start with Smarketing.

More on Points and Scoring

Another important component to smarketing efficiency was introduced in Chapter 8. The scoring of leads, helps the sales team to focus efforts on the leads that they are most likely to convert into clients or customers. These are the leads that are qualified, interested, and ready to take action. As previously explained, using a system of points and scoring helps your sales team to know where to focus their efforts and when. This way time is not wasted on a prospect who hasn't been engaged enough yet to be ready for an offer or opportunity. Your sales team has limitations of time available to connect with each prospect in your funnel. If they only focus on the prospects that are most likely to take action, then their time is being used in the best way to serve the company.

Again, the key to creating a successful lead scoring/points system is to integrate with the sales team at the early stages of creating your sales funnel lead program. The sales team is in the best position to reveal what demographics, features, experiences, or actions, result in the best sales leads with highest conversions. They can also provide insight into activities that are good indicators that a prospect is getting closer to making a decision.

As mentioned previously, a point system could resemble something like this:

- You can have leads go through a funnel

with a point system.

- Once they reach 100 points, only then they are qualified to send to the sales team.
- A possible point breakdown could be - opening the third email would earn them 50 points, responding is a further 50 points = 100 points.
- The goal is to incorporate actions that are more likely associated with sales quality leads. Your sales team are the best resource to help your company determine what are the most common indicators that a prospective customer is close to making a decision.
- Your points scoring system will reflect a typical score that measures lead movement from TOFU (the Top of the Sales Funnel), to MOFU (Marketing Qualified lead, and then BOFU (bottom of the sales funnel – where the prospect becomes a customer). This can also be reflected as a progression from stranger to friend to customer.

When the marketing strategy team, works with the sales team, the chances of operating an efficient sales system, improve substantially. And this is the best way to assure that all of the benefits of an effective inbound strategy are not wasted due to a poor follow-up system.

Smarketing strategies are also critical to a business' Return on Investment (ROI). Smarketing assures that the entire marketing and sales team members are operating at peak efficiency and all resources are cultivated in a timely manner to drive maximum results.

Chapter 10
Converting Leads
into Clients

No matter how many "qualified" leads your Inbound Marketing campaigns yield, they are worthless if you can't convert them into clients. From the content that first attracts your target market, through the building of trust and a relationship, to the decision of your target to become a customer – your entire customer journey must be mapped out and planned.

The Customer Journey

With your Customer Persona in hand, you should first determine the topics that your potential clients, need to hear. You need to define their core values and objectives. And you need to have a very clear understanding of what matters to them and what problems they need solutions to.

Now that you know what they want to know, you and your team can start creating content on a consistent basis. The best way to do this properly is with a content calendar and a content planner. To help you prepare these, I have included the *Inbound Marketing Launch Tools* section on page 87. Start to build a list of potential topics and delivery content formats. Then map out at least a month in advance, all of the content that needs to be created and when it will be released, posted, or shared. Your content production operation must be organized, consistent, and relevant in order to be an effective driver of results.

This is also a good time to remember the lessons learned on creating relevant content that provides solutions to your prospects' challenges and needs. Know what your ideal clients want, need, and care about and then create content that addresses their specific concerns. If your content is relevant to your prospects, then it might be the first opportunity for them to discover your company and to learn about your lead magnet.

The Irresistible Lead Magnet & Conversion Offer
All of your team's created content should include an offer that brings value to your clients. Make it as irresistible and useful as possible, so that they are more likely to take action and that first step into your sales funnel. Once a prospect takes that first step toward your business the clock starts ticking. That initial new "lead" must be acted on within ONE HOUR to yield the best outcome. In a study conducted by a Graduate school professor[1], leads that were acted on within an hour were 7X more likely to result in an engaging interaction, moving the prospect further along on the customer journey into your sales funnel. After 24 hours pass, the chances of having a meaningful engagement drops considerably. Each of your leads are valuable and should be treated that way. In some cases, this may mean that your autoresponder will deliver the requested lead magnet within the hour. In other situations, it may

---

[1] https://hbr.org/2011/03/the-short-life-of-online-sales-leads

mean that a prospect that fills out a web form inquiry, will receive a call from your response team or automated response within that first hour.

Your ongoing content creation and engagement opportunities must continue to provide mini-solutions and progressive answers for your target group. Your clients want to get from Point A to Point B. Your job is to help them to continue to get closer toward their Point B. This is the stage where your leads begin to know, like, and trust you as a credible resource to help them achieve their Point B.

It is then time to present an offer to the leads that are near the BOFU (bottom of the sales funnel). This offer must also be irresistible. Assuming your marketing efforts are efficient in building relationships with your true target market, then it is imperative to know and understanding what your prospects are ready to buy and the best way to pitch it to them. This might be an opportunity to sample your product or service at a lower price point or it might be the chance to have an enhanced experience with your company. Either way, it is critical to design your offer to match the needs and wishes of your target market.

Delighting Clients – Creating Evangelists
Once a lead becomes a customer, your marketing responsibilities are NOT over. It is then time to DELIGHT your new clients. All of your company efforts to provide amazing after-purchase customer service will become the true differentiators. It is how you treat your new clients that will define your brand's reputation and

customer loyalty. Even more important, it is from your new customer base that you can identify and nurture potential brand evangelists.

Brand evangelists are an invaluable asset to your company. They are customers that are so enthusiastic about your company, product, or brand, that they actively and enthusiastically talk about and share info about your company, product, or service. Evangelists are not "happy customers" they are "ecstatic customers." Brand evangelists create new customers through their enthusiastic sharing of your company's details.

Some of the most effective ways to find and nurture brand evangelists is to create unique opportunities for engagement. Surveys, social media posts, share buttons are good starters. The key is to monitor and respond. When you acknowledge retweets and helpful comments about your company or you respond to a happy customer's comprehensive feedback, you help to create super fans that feel special and rewarded. It is also helpful to provide exclusive "extras" for those customers that enthusiastically push your brand and messaging. This could be a first peek or early access to new products or services. It can also be exclusive experiences that give your evangelists special access opportunities.

So, as you may now realize, Inbound Marketing starts a process that turns strangers into friends and then friends into customers. And if you're really lucky (or strategic) some customers will become super fans or evangelists.

"People don't buy what you do, they buy why you do it."
– Simon Sinek

There is one additional concept needs to be an important part of your entire marketing equation. That is, as explained by author and Top TED Talk lecturer, Simon Sinek[2], *"people don't buy what you do, they buy why you do it."* That's an extremely powerful understanding of what attracts people to you and your company. So, don't be shy about your why. Make sure that the people you want to appeal to, understand your mission, vision, and purpose. If they understand and appreciate your "why" they will most certainly find the inbound path that you created to help them find you.

---

[2] https://www.ted.com/speakers/simon_sinek

Inbound Marketing Launch Tools

To help you prepare your Inbound Marketing campaigns, I have provided some worksheets and checklists to help you manage and maintain your promotions.

Tools included:

- ➢ Customer Persona Worksheet
- ➢ Sales Funnel Planner
- ➢ Content Calendar
- ➢ Content Creation Planner

Custom Persona Worksheet

Customer Persona Worksheet

Insert Image

DEMOGRAPHICS (age, marital status, occupation, gender, family details, geographic location, income, etc.)

BACKGROUND/BIOGRAPHY
(Education, life milestones, his/her story.)

PSYCHOGRAPHICS, IDENTIFIERS, GOALS, HOBBIES, INTERESTS, & ACTIVITIES

CHALLENGES, PAIN POINTS, & NEEDS

COMMON OBJECTIONS, FEARS, & REASONS THEY BECAME or MIGHT BECOME A CUSTOMER

Sales Funnel Planner
(The Customer Journey)

Sales Funnel Planner

Target Market:

Their problem or need:

Your product/service solution:

Useful Lead Magnet:

Engagement Plans:

Your Offer:

Plan to Delight Your Customers:

Content Calendar
(1 Week Plan)

Date	Topic Theme	Content Title	Content Type	Offer CTA	Posted Shared
1					
2					
3					
4					
5					
6					
7					

Content Calendar
(Holidays/Special Events)

Month	Note any special days that can be used as a tie in to your subject matter or topics
Jan	
Feb	
Mar	
Apr	
May	
Jun	
Jul	
Aug	
Sep	
Oct	
Nov	
Dec	

Content Calendar
(Holidays/Special Events Reference Sites)

- https://en.wikipedia.org/wiki/Lists_of_holidays

- https://en.wikipedia.org/wiki/List_of_unofficial_o
  bservances_by_date

- https://en.wikipedia.org/wiki/List_of_commemora
  tive_days

- https://www.timeanddate.com/holidays/

- https://www.brownielocks.com/month2.html

- https://www.hospitals.healthgrades.com/hospitals
  /blog/2018-healthcare-observances-calendar

- https://healthfinder.gov/NHO/

- https://militarybenefits.info/military-calendar-
  holidays-events-observances/

- https://nationaldaycalendar.com/calendar-at-a-
  glance/

Content Creation Planner

What is the problem or challenge that your product or service solves?

_____

_____

_____

_____

The following are some of the most common types of content that can be easily created to connect with your market. Start to brainstorm and list some topics or ideas that would work well for the following types of content. What information would be helpful to your potential clients? Keep in mind, that any idea or content piece in one format, can be easily repurposed in other content type categories.

Audio content

_____

_____

_____

_____

_____

Blog posts and articles

_____

_____

_____

_____

_____

_____

Case studies

_____

_____

_____

_____

_____

Checklists

_____

_____

_____

_____

_____

Ebooks

_____

_____

_____

_____

_____

Infographics & images

_____

_____

_____

_____

_____

Slide presentations

Research reports

Social media posts

Teleseminars

Templates

_____
_____
_____
_____
_____
_____

Videos

_____
_____
_____
_____
_____

Webinars

_____
_____
_____
_____
_____

White papers

_____
_____
_____
_____
_____

Worksheets and lesson sheets

Closing Thoughts

Inbound Marketing can and will transform your business providing you with more opportunities to connect with the target market groups you hope to serve.

Your Inbound Marketing will be driven by the content your company creates to connect with your target market groups. Your content must be relevant, and it must pertain to the things that matter to your prospects.

So, here is timeless advice from an advertising legend:

"Make it simple.
Make it memorable.
Make it inviting to look at.
Make it fun to read."
-Leo Burnett

About the Author
Patrick Bugeja

For Patrick Bugeja, getting involved in internet businesses, happened quite by accident. His fascination with the internet all started as a hobby. Initially he started building simple webpages and applying SEO and AdWords. Then, his business owner friends started asking him to do the same for them. When these business owners offered to pay for services that Patrick previously did as his hobby, things started to get more interesting.

Soon, Patrick was getting steady business and word of mouth marketing started to take over. He clearly had a new part-time business happening. However, it wasn't until he was offered a position at a Marketing Agency that he started to expand on a big scale.

Patrick's new employer allowed Patrick to develop his new office's online presence. Patrick soon after, realized that, helping others to optimize their marketing strategy, online activities, and ad performance was his passion. And that's when Intraforce Marketing was borne.

Today, Intraforce Marketing helps companies by connecting them to the many valuable partnerships, that can support and propel them, with the best fit possible. Intraforce Marketing's vision is to build a credible database of partnerships that can assist with products and services across a broad range of industries.

Intraforce is building communities via social media to keep members in touch and informed at all times with ideas, tools, and services that members can offer to each other, turning an industrial battle into a unity of one with a vision of an unbreakable foundation.

How Intraforce Can Help You Launch a Successful Inbound Marketing Enterprise

You are invited to join our community of like minded entrepreneurs who are ready to take charge of their online aspirations and build a solid and successful business.

When you join the Intraforce Mastermind Facebook group you'll be connected to resources, tools, networking, and coaching to help you maximize your business potential. Our community of new and seasoned entrepreneurs are a unified force and foundation aimed at supporting and guiding members to achieve business success.

Go to:
http://www.facebook.com/groups/IntraforceMastermindGroup
to join the Intraforce Mastermind Facebook Group
today!

Image Credits

Images featured in Customer Persona examples from Pixabay.

Gold Medal Flour ad Image
Public Domain,
https://commons.wikimedia.org/w/index.php?curid=1893309

Gold Medal Flour Picture ad
Public Domain,
https://commons.wikimedia.org/w/index.php?curid=1890488

At Five this day Carriage
By Internet Archive Book Images -
https://www.flickr.com/photos/internetarchivebookimages/14783499712/
Source book page:
https://archive.org/stream/historyofadverti00samp/historyofadverti00sam
p#page/n518/mode/1up
No restrictions,
https://commons.wikimedia.org/w/index.php?curid=44189562

Ads on walls of train station 1874=Henry Sampson
By Sampson, Henry, 1841-1891 -
https://www.flickr.com/photos/internetarchivebookimages/14783833545/
Source book page:
https://archive.org/stream/historyofadverti00samp/historyofadverti00sam
p#page/n13/mode/1up
, No restrictions,
https://commons.wikimedia.org/w/index.php?curid=42610553

Blouse Ad – LA Herald 1917
https://commons.wikimedia.org/w/index.php?title=File:Los_Angeles_Her
ald,_Number_100,_26_February_1917.pdf&page=2

Drug Shop – Egyptian Bazaar
https://commons.wikimedia.org/wiki/File:A_drug_shop_in_the_Egyptian
_bazaar,_Constantinople._Oil_pain_Wellcome_V0023495.jpg
Hatshepsut Egyptian trading Expedition

*https://commons.wikimedia.org/wiki/File:Relief_of_Hatshepsut%27s_exp
edition_to_the_Land_of_Punt_by_%CE%A3%CF%84%CE%B1%CF%
8D%CF%81%CE%BF%CF%82.jpg*

*old tv
https://pixabay.com/en/old-retro-television-tubes-tv-1299417/*

*spam mail box
https://pixabay.com/en/spam-mail-box-email-3d-render-sign-2636258/*

*social media
https://pixabay.com/en/online-internet-icon-symbols-www-942402/*

*making cake
https://pixabay.com/en/retro-vintage-home-cake-dessert-1291738/*

*vintage-mom-baby
https://pixabay.com/en/vintage-woman-girl-female-lady-1319058/*

*idea 1
https://pixabay.com/en/bright-bulb-career-climbing-light-2855120/*

*Problem
https://pixabay.com/en/problem-solution-help-support-2731501/*

*content tree
https://pixabay.com/en/tree-social-media-structure-1148032/*

*mktg strategy
https://pixabay.com/en/marketing-strategies-3105875/*

*face / social media
https://pixabay.com/en/woman-face-head-question-mark-241327/*

*chess
https://pixabay.com/en/chess-strategy-chess-board-316658/*

*Puzzle piece hand
https://pixabay.com/en/connect-jigsaw-strategy-1586220/*

people puzzle
https://pixabay.com/en/team-businessmen-cooperation-2651913/

inbound arrows
https://pixabay.com/en/arrows-inside-pressure-request-2029157/

question head
https://pixabay.com/en/question-question-mark-survey-2736480/

search globe
https://pixabay.com/en/globe-planet-search-loupe-158146/

social picture icons
https://pixabay.com/en/icon-polaroid-blogger-rss-tumblr-2486501/

click here
https://pixabay.com/en/hand-click-click-here-finger-1367819/

robot face
https://pixabay.com/en/girl-forward-digital-digitization-2181709/

woman – VR glasses
https://pixabay.com/en/clouds-female-game-girl-model-1845517/

man at arrows board
https://pixabay.com/en/board-arrows-decision-right-next-2084777/

Sales Funnel Image – Courtesy of https://www.listshack.com/image-collection
https://www.flickr.com/photos/152123747@N06/32863956976

Brain Bulb
https://pixabay.com/en/anatomy-axons-biology-brain-bright-2952567/